# A Pilgrim

and 20 other poems

Poornima Dayal

BookLeaf Publishing

India | USA | UK

Made with ❤ on the BookLeaf Publishing Platform
www.bookleafpub.in
www.bookleafpub.com

# Dedication

I dedicate this book of poems to the Almighty and thank Him profusely.

# Preface

Poetry is a vast, seamless piece of imagination.
This book 'A Pilgrim', includes 21 poems, which talk
about my travels to holy places as well as life's certain
learnings. These poems also elaborate a feeling of
harmony.
With an imaginative and romantic touch to most to
them, I have tried to convey my internal journey.
Some of them are visual treats and delights about places
visited.


Hope the readers enjoy this bunch of poems which
I dedicate as a bouquet of flowers to The Almighty.
Thanks for picking it up.

# Acknowledgements

I am grateful to the Almighty for helping me through life
and its journey.
I thank my son, my husband, my mother and loving pet
for always being so supportive.

# 1. Radha Krishna

'Radhe Radhe', Radhe Radhe
Krishna Krishna,
sing along and praise the Lord
his mellifluous flute and each of its chord.

Those big, transparent eyes so pure
watching, guiding on paths so sure.
Truth prevails, only truth prevails
the only reality to inhale.
Lips so tender and hands so soft,
draped in Velvet cloaks with Copper dots.
Wise is he who listens to Thee
lucky is he who gets to see
those luminous, big eyes
that speak no lies
Only truth prevails - only truth prevails.

Oh Krishna, my Krishna, as I call
you hold and caress, lest I fall.
Those unconditional vibes

that best describe
your magnitude
the length of every longitude
the very breath of all latitude.
The universe, the world all one
every country, grassland town and city
in living beings, in every nitty gritty.

Unfathomable, perennial and everlasting
The only truth that prevails
where every ship of life sails.
Seamless, imperial and royal
Oh Krishna, a cry from Thou slave
to keep me in prayer and always loyal.

# 2. The Rama Idol

You are bathed in splendour
MariGold garlands and Petunias I render.
The majestic bow and Golden arrow,
a Diamond necklace with glittering edges
and delicately weaved drapes with lace cut into wedges.

'Jai Shri Ram', as they shout with fervour
waiting am I to be Thy server.
As they instal Your idol so unique and fine
witnessing such magnanimity, the pleasure is all mine.

The sculptor, a blessed soul
plays such an important role
with such dexterity engraving every piece of stone
in ways that none can ever clone.
Such a marvel, bringing so much joy
such amazement at this site to enjoy.

Saffron robes of priests alike
singing hymns and songs with utter delight.
Welcoming the Lord, in this installation
the bells tolling, causing a devotional vibration.

Thronging in thousands are pilgrims from far and wide
offering sweets and bounties without any divide.
A child snuggled in his mother's lap
awaiting a glimpse and till then he naps.
A Wheatish young woman with that Silvery nose ring
holding a basket and Vermilion strings,
some ripe Gauvas and Berries in the basket she brings.
That couple, in love as they may seem
hustling, jostling to reach The Supreme
holding hands, one behind the other
as they make way through the bar and beam
coming to life is their remarkable dream.

His face is gleaming
blessing each passer by
as they venerate, letting out a devotional cry.
I thank and bow
amazed at such glory
beyond any book or it's story.

Praise be to Lord.
Exalt The Lord.

Adoration to God.

Thanks to God.

# 3. The Divine Mother

Nestled In the cosy lap of Trikuta Hills,
a little above the pious valleys of Katra,
above those plains and plateaus of Jammu
are you located, oh, my Mother so holy.
A visit to Thou is ever refreshing, always restoring us so
wholly.

Approaching the base camp
with surreal lit lamps
with many soldiers at guard like wonder Champs
is this little dwelling
my peaceful setting
where I hear temple sounds soothingly belling.

Awaiting that morning when heli's may fly
when the skies are clear and no body can deny.
A trip upto the Goddess with Her magnanimous Shine
blessing us always is Her sacred, blessed Shrine.
I bow, revere, offering my self
walking, at times halting into this pious journey I delve.

No copter, they say
today is no day.
It's raining
It's pouring
with clouds asunder.
predicted for the day
as there may be thunder.

Holding his hands, I begin my walk
as so many pilgrims flock.
Ponies and horses, some grazy white and Charcoal black,
rustic looking Horsemen with peppered beards and olive
slacks.

Devotees are millions
thronging in zillions.
Subtle murmers of rhythmic chants,
little children and parents with their uncle n aunts.
A climb filled with fervour and devotion divine
as people climb up through mountains and ravines.

Making my way up
thanking with earnest
for this gift so special, it is the best.
Redeemed am I
oh my Mother.
Submitted am I

oh my mother.
Approaching Thy temple
is ever so real
so healing and genuinely ideal.
Salutations, my Master,
my celestial mother
how else may I chant Thy name
know not for I am just so lame.
In Gratitude for Thy mercies
asking for pardon, a life devoid of controversies.
Grants and boons do I seek
for know not much as I am meek.

Nestled In the cosy lap of Trikuta Hills
a little above the pious valleys of Katra,
above those plains and plateaus of Jammu
are you located, oh, my mother so holy.
A visit to Thou is forever
refreshing us always so wholly.

# 4. Cinema

There are movies and there are more
the sizzle, sparkle and fantasies galore.
Telling tales of cities and characters from the folklore
of dwellings, habitations and musty shores.

'All we imagine as light', The White Tiger', 'Anuja' and so
many more
making it to the Oscars or almost so.
Of love and lover's from fables bygone,
of soldiers and warriors - those mighty heroes,
those thrilling vibes or distresful throes.
Cinema, is thy name universal
where heroes and heroines perform many a rehearsals.

The big screen they say, is full of grime n dust
intresting stories to tell of stars and starlets.
The glamor this industry holds
appears to make the country mould
into humans or beasts
as the tale may be told.

Never ending, creative passions
flaming the fires of director's and other hire's.
Such crowds never were seen
in magnum releases,
in big budget movies
with celebrated actors
and all those involved contractors.

Fancy - fancy, delights and treats
at openings in decorated, charming retreats.
Pshusia pinks and Tinsel Reds
those twinkling lights like a bed of starlit threads.

Dream again baby for its lacy and juicy
this story of villains and damsels is so very meaty.
Blockbusters or nothing less are they called
rocking the charts, as audiences they hold enthralled.

The sober yet intense Oscar nominations
different from the so called above denominations.
Messengers in their own rights
fruitful and appreciated
with humble casts
yet a script well initiated.

TV or be it the Otp,

the big screen world
or the stage with curtains twirled.
A reality or a fictional illusion
nonetheless, is worth all the infusion.

# 5. Sign of Love

The pounding of my heart, I felt
like my swift, galloping horse Roosevelt.
A sign of love, of being in love
with some one known or perhaps yet unknown.
A wave of love floats
not a passing fancy am sure
but some long lasting friendship to lure.

Is it love, I wonder
or a sign from yonder.

Mysterious, yet, truly lovable
an inspiration, a sensation
beyond words of explanation.
A subtle joy, hoping it's forever
but know not I, for I am not so clever.

Gazing at The Divine, a moment of glance
asking, thanking for this awesome chance.
Whoever he may be, search I not afar

some one close
whom He chose.
Some people come in life to show
and it is just so good to know
what love is all about to us
where we stand and how we may glow.
Gratifying channels of sheer romance
sharing, holding hands to dance.
Inexplicable and heart warmingly ethereal
explaining the unity between the so called unreal and
real.

There is no screen
no veil nor shadow
such transparent love
straight from his heart perhaps,
naturally holy and devoid of gaps.

Thanking Thee, I look above
for helping me always in cherishing this love.

# 6. A Pilgrim

My romance is with you alone
Only me for you to own.
I am but a pilgrim here
a visit to this land that is fair.
With passersby, few trespassers
with dance, music and a melodious harper.
Moving as I do from town to town
meeting loving people but few who frown.
Experiencing those so called life learnings
helping me write and express these jottings.
Pilgrim am I, of these magical pastures
living till you decide my time for departure.
Traveling through holy lands and temples
wearing White and Saffron, cotton ensembles.
Partaking of nourishing foods and delights
consecrated by Thy love and light.

A pilgrim am I.....traveling through holy lands.

Of sadhus and sanyasis is my hometown
in my heart, my vision as I lie down.
Breathing, chanting thus, your name
reminiscing the glow of the holy flame.
Magnolia essence and Rose insence
wafting, weaving their way across
using them diligently is what I endorse.
Frankincense filling up the room
being a pilgrim is such a boon.
At night time do I gaze at the enchanting Moon
with folded hands do I croon
a song, a Godly verse or two
liening on my cot as the moonlight peeps through.

A pilgrim am I... traveling through holy lands.

Transient is life, and it's many factors
relishing, accepting I am just an actor.
On this stage called life I revolve and dance
like a ballerina whose got this special chance
to live, enjoy and so call learn
to imagine, paint and thence earn.

A pilgrim am I.....traveling through holy lands.

Counting stars and days and nights
worshiping the Sun God

thanking the might of the Lord
moving through places at His every nod.
The journey must go on they say
and time ticks by from December to May.
Each year, each month bringing in fresh flowers,
come summer, spring and some monsoon showers.
Soothing tired bodies and minds alike,
blossoming Jasmine, lillies and lotus that we like
enjoying crispy vegetable fritters and roasted corn as we
travel on our bike.

Moving ahead on Earth as we do
from mind to heart and body, it's so true.

A pilgrim am I.......traveling through holy lands.

# 7. Hare Krishna

Lift me upto you,
hug me tight and feel me through
for you are the absolute, only truth.
An illetrate passer, as I am
of this world, of many a woman and man.
Just your mercy is enough
when life brings moments that may seem tough.
Gaping at Thy mighty form
to ward away unnecessary worry or storm.
Way forward, is the only way
not looking back, as you say nay.

Mounted horses, mountains and peaks
clad in blankets of Silvery snow
as white as a very old men's brow.
Living in hotels and
sundry, tiny motels
with airy windows
and wooden beds,
with quilted sheds

made of woolen threads.

Gushing Blue waters,
from every quarter.
Fresh, cold streams and pretty, clear brooklets
meandering through steep hilly slopes
viewing this dream am I, so full of hope.
With joyful visions and abundant treasuries,
with fiery passions and endearing memories,
enjoying colourful fantasies and happy reveries.

Oh Krishna, my savior
the doer of our lives !
Who am I to know more
bathed in Thy love as it sores.
Hey Krishna, lift me upto you
Hey Krishna , lift me up to you.
Pray I, this very soul
to take me away from all that's supposedly foul
happy to be just that little foal
eating from Thy hands and the holy bowl
that's all I know for there ain't any other real goal.
Ho Krishna Ho Krishna.
Hare Hare.

# 8. Tubby - The Siamese Cat

Tubby, the podgy Siamese cat
Black n White,
with fuzzy fur, shinning so bright.
Twirling and rolling around her belly
just after its bath, it's no longer smelly.

Purring and stirring then lieing in my arms
twisting and turning, in those Silver Oak Farms.
As it hugs,
I feel a tug
of warmth and subtle breathing whispers
as I gently touch, petting it's silky whiskers.
A mix of white and shimmery cream,
this love is so unconditional and so it seems.

Tubby- Tubby it's time for supper
to relish nanny's hearty fish soup
as she coyly stoops
pouring into your cobalt, Steel bowl
that steamed Tuna and some sticky Chicken roll.

Waking up, slowly as it walks
towards her meal
leaving me to watch on my phone some crazy reels.
'Tubby', I shout, though lovingly
'wait, am coming' , I speak gushingly.

Under the moonlit night,
a night to remember
when her eyes were Green and flashed like Amber.
That twinkle, that grin surpassing all wit
with cats and dogs does this world get lit.
Lets Serenade to music and let us dance
let me hold those supple paws, as you prance.
Holding my hands, her nimble, furry paws
with manicured nails, just like her friend Shaw's.
'Like a virgin', playing on the stereo
is Maddona's famous song,
in the province of Ontario,
as we dance so long.
Tubby- tubby, it's a night to remember
for it's mid month, it's a warm September.

My darling, I croon
I will get you married soon
to Shaw or the likes
on a tall mountain when we go on our hikes.

Oh, Tubby my podgy siamese cat.

# 9. Museum

The museum, as gorgeous as it were
palatial with walls so White
with hanging artworks and objects of delight.
Tourists coming in numbers
with their fathers and mothers,
youngsters and best friends
dressed in their best, following the latest trends.

Those diligently carved stone sculptures
to paintings of hunters,
of horses and horse riders
to peasants and farmers.
With dots and squares
to ceremonious fairs
of vintage eras
and Tchaikovsky's operas.
That long Blue painting
with pointed leaves and water,
that huge, Earthen pot
crafted by some well known potter.

The bright, open windows
through which Sunlight shows.
Those tall, grand ceilings
and enormous art rooms
with plenty of artefacts
and priceless heirlooms.

In the city of New York is this fascinating art museum
with varied pictures of religious mausoleums.
Ironically, situated amidst those harsh city walls
occupying vast spaces and large, brilliant halls.

# 10. Mahashivratri

With Mahashivratri approaching thus
with crowds thronging planes and bus,
making their way to Varanasi, Ujjain and Mount
Kailasha
since time immemorial and when there were saints like
Vyasa[1]
the celestial night in Phalgun Masa[2].

The Marriage of heavenly Lord Shiva and Parvati
bedecked with twinkling jewels, in plush silken robes
with Emerald and Ruby studded earrings around their
ear lobes.
Singing praises of them is the Skanda Purana[3],
worshiping with reverence in the Lingam Purana[4],
as written is also above in the Lotus Purana[5].

The night of His sureal Tandav Nritaya[6]
creating, Preserving and destroying

as every devotee sings truly enjoying.
Fasting, meditating and dancing through night and day
mists and Sandal fragrances do they spray.

A blissful wedding is commemorated
his passionate dance being venerated
on the hindu date of Magha Chaturdash[7]
when pilgrims leave for temples in a rush.
Burning oil lamps and cubes of Camphor,
with bhasma[8] and Sandal pastes is filled their hamper.
In Somenath, Dharmasthala and Murudeshwara
are sights to watch as people worship their favorite
Ishwara[9].

Oh my Neelkantha, my Mahadeva, Maheshwara
oh my ever enchanting Jagdeshwara.
Holding hands of his consort Bhavani[10],
my very mother Durga[11], Bhavya[12], Gauri[13] and
Shivani[14].
His beloved and forever lovable
Devi[15], Sharda[16] or Amba[17],
a night to remember and chant Jagdamba[18].
With perseverance her penance she performed
winning his heart so deeply warmed.
From Sati[19] to Goddess Parvati was she born
for us to worship and help us reform.

A night to remember and never forget
captivating, charming and forever dazzling
as we rejoice and celebrate with all engaging
recitals and programs are bhaktas[20] staging.

------------------------------------------------------------------

------------------------------------------------------------------

------------------------

1.Traditionally regarded as the compiler of the Mantras
in the Vedas into 4 texts.
2.12th, final month of Hindu Calendar.
3.Hindu religious text where Skanda is considered a son
of Lord Shiva and Goddess Parvati.
4.Hindu religious text where Linga is considered to be
the iconographical symbol for Lord Shiva.
5.Hindu religious text. Lotus is considered to be offered
to Lord Shiva for spiritual growth.
6.The Divine dance of Lord Shiva.
7.14th day of the dark half of the Magh month in Hindu
Calendar.
8.Sacred ash used in Hindu rituals.
9.Another name for the Lord.
10.Another name of Goddess Parvati
11.Another name for Goddess Parvati.
12. Another name forGoddess Parvati.
13. Another name for Lord Shiva's wife Parvati.

14. Another name for Goddess Parvati.

15. Another name for Goddess Parvati.

16. Another name for Goddess Parvati.

17. Another name for Goddess Parvati.

18. Another name for Goddess Parvati.

19. Another name for Goddess Parvati.

20. Devotees.

# 11. The Golden temple

Waheguru - Waheguru - Waheguru[1]
Satnam[2] Waheguru.
Hoping to visit the shrine again
this magnificent temple helps us regain
our zest for life and a purpose to move on
great devotion within us is born.
In the sacred Santorum where the holy book rests
giving us blessings and love at its best.
Under the moonlit skies, on a starry night
by the glorious waters, the temple glowing so bright.
A shimmering Blue
is the waters hue
as I continue walking in the mile long queue.

With head covered in Red and Yellow
I sing and hum in a voice so mellow.
My friends ahead and behind
of His sublimity do they remind
chanting and praising

with voices raising
slogans of love and devotion
as the queue is in motion.


An open house of worship for all people alike
with packed crowds from all walks of life.
The holy water tanks
amongst the most unique do they rank.
What a site, a visit so pristine
before the Lord and the 'Gurugranthsahib'[3] do we lean.
Begging, asking for pardon
softening our hearts that may by now be hardened.
.

The Golden shawl draping the Holiness
it's Seams and body dressed in White pearls
with lace and embroidery stitched by some girls
working dexterously as they do
singing holy verses
and some devotionally written holy phrases
devout, sincere and loyal people
working on the shawl with a thick needle.


Loving hands serving food
with milk and rice and Semolina stewed.
Tasty lentils and cooked Potatoes
leafy vegetables with Red, ripe Tomatoes
The scenes on site

are filled with light
under the Moon or under the Sun
praying, revering are children having fun.


Waheguru, Waheguru as I speak and move
as feelings of piety within me groove
it's truly a dance
of being in trance.
The divine waters as I sip,
words and greetings are on each one's lips.


Waheguru - Satnam - Waheguru Satnam.

--------------------------------------------------------------------------

--------------------------------------------------------------------------

-----------------------


1.Term used in Sikkhism to refer to God.
2.True name
3.The holy Sikh book.

# 12. Live and let live

Life ain't a method or a methodology
it's neither History, Physics nor Biology.
There ain't a need to analyse human Psychology.
Just live, enjoy and let live is the only triology.

Don't try and see what's beyond
of knowing the unknown why are you fond?.
There's no restriction
no jurisdiction
just some beliefs
giving some weird reliefs.
Hold not thyself to punish
let bygones be, just flourish.

Accepting what's on
just let it bring on
mowing your own lawn
since the time of dawn.
A garden to remember
of which we are all members

temporary, not static
there's just nothing so enigmatic.

Letting go a need to dwell and drill
to know every bit of the fancy and frill
embracing the now, enjoying it's thrill
keeping it low, not making a mountain or hill.

Live and let live is the only motto I know
loving its moments, being in the flow
relishing God's great gifts that He mercifully bestows
loving each dog, cat, cattle n crow.
There's just no need to make many friends or foe
thanking the Lord for our body, each organ n toe.
Holding His hands as we gently walk in a row.

Live and let live is the only motto I know
no interference,
no adherence to rules or laws
binding mankind in their rowdy claws.
A day full of gratitude
a positive attitude,
a night of quietitude
sprinkled with moments of solitude,
an evening of thankful prayers of immense magnitude.

Live and let live is the only motto I know.

# 13. Mother Nature

Birds fly close and far
merrily do I watch them from my car.
Some Alabastrine white, some baby fawn
soaring ever since dawn.
Innocent with no guile,
criss crossing the skies with their pretty smiles.

Adults and babies, flying across,
on my way to the church to worship the Holy Cross.
Following my path or is it reverse
as I pull out my camera from my purse.
Clicking such delightful sights
is within my democratic rights
another passion so pleasing
this moment on camera am I freezing.

Their song so soft and sweet
perhaps, something I should now tweet.
In this world of social media
where we need not an encyclopedia.

Like a Nightingale's lullaby
like a cheerful swan song
lyrics I haven't heard since time so long.
Their beaks are Pinkish, Green
with an irresistible glow and sheen
like never before have I ever seen.

Hurrah- Hurrah, am on my way
whilst enjoying a lengthy bird trail
as I quietly and surely inhale and exhale.
The surrounding hillocks
what a glorious sight
with subtle peaks and plataued heights
as I make way to the holy Mount.Mary
hungry am I but not so weary
gazing at them quenches my thirst
reaching my destination to let my feelings burst.

Birds of paradise, I say
dancing in circles
around the Bandra circle
around few Red stones and tiny girdles.
Nature - Nature
Thy be so luring
blossoming and blooming as you be alluring.

Flowers and birds dancing and gleaming
as I approach the church, utter delight am I feeling.

# 14. Frangipani

Remembering the Frangipani tree
outside an old home did it grow for free.
Watching it sprout from babyhood to adulthood
blossoming as well as it should.

Plumeria, it's scientific name
decorating the hair of many a dame.
Deciduous in nature with latex in sap
flowering abundantly, around the branches as they wrap.
Some Yellowish - White or brightly Pink
watching them grow at my every blink.
With fragments of Jasmine, Citrus and Gardenia
growing in the soil right next to radiant and festive
Petunia.
These highly fragrant flowers, especially at night
seem to always grow so wonderfully bright.
Dancing and moving as the swift winds blow
walking around them in the evenings a bit slow.
Breathing in their intense essence
as they cheerfully made me feel their presence.

Mixing with the flowing air
their slightly Vanilla smell is to share
as gently did I walk around them always, without any
care.
Watching them Grow at the end of their stems in
clusters
walking and listening as I did to melodious chart
busters.
Frangipani my friends, always inspiring
as I mentally weave poetry, lightly prespiring.
Plucking them may be a sin
but offering them at the Altar I did with with a grin.
A small, fleshy tree
growing in full spree
observing them as I did when I was ever free.

Their notable sweet smell
with Roses do they gel
rising above the ground they do so well.

Frangipani, my friend
you will always be in trend
for temples and homes alike
as women and men do always like
taking you for worship
even when the airs got a slight nip.

# 15. Mr. Rimps

A delectable salad with Walnuts and Avocados
a treat for those salad loving aficionados
with little cocktail Shrimps
a favorite with one Monsieur Christiphor Rimps.


His voluminous Blonde moustache
marinated with mushy Apple dressing
as he slurped and licked the fruit while pressing .
Of Bananas and Berries was a thick shake
without which he wouldn't this salad ever take
with dexterous hands when he did make
this salad and beverage that he could
partake.


Roasted duck glazed with Primrose oil
made under pressures of heat with great toil
wrapped and plastered in layers with shinny Aluminium
foil
dressed with fragrant Raspberries veiled under lightly
Green Voil.

A burly, rich man
sitting under his roof and fan
with his radiant wife Lina
in the Pampas of Argentina.
Where temperatures are moderate
and the rainy waters evenly precipate.

Enjoying a rich harvest,
in his bold White Vest
did seem to meditate
before he ever ate
his plate full of goodies
worthy of such loving foodies.

Mr.Rimps did always sing
wearing his fancy and year old ring
made of Turquoise and Rubies that shine
reflecting the light across his glass of wine.

Of love and laughter was his story
a man who wrote about nobles and past history.
Believing in love was his only theory
prayed as he to the Lord's bountiful glory.

# 16. Live on I will...

Live on I will ..
The facade that exists or is it a veil,
come what may I won't care for such hail
when I am young or even if I ever get frail.

No longer am I mute, allowing my expressions to speak
No permissions do I any longer seek.
Out of a shell or that comforted womb
into my own with a bang and boom
with memories buried in forgotten tombs
to make new, happy ones now there is enough room.
Finally out of that sheltered cocoon
ready are new designs and stories to weave on a fresh
loom.

Tear me you can't
for never will I part
from who I am or
where I am.
This is my story

and live on I will
no hurt, no grief can now instill.
No pain, no blame
no manipulated behaviors
may ever play there part
till heavens decide my time to depart.

Ha- Ha - Ha , I laugh and joke
at words spoken by some past folks
while whipping frothy Whites and few Golden egg yolks.
They carry no weight, no longer it seems
enjoying this victory I joyfully scream.
Walking out of its grip was actually easy
holding hands of my Lord, made it so breezy.

Painting my best
in my cosy, warm nest
I now certainly rest.
This is my story
and live on I will .....

# 17. Living in the moment

Live in the moment
no fret of tomorrow or dayafter.
Just live in the moment
live and enjoy
there's nothing to bother or destroy.
Just this moment so dear
when your loved ones are near
and there's nothing to fear.

Thanking each moment
there's nothing to lament
just learning to love and be in the present.
Embrace and laugh
there's nothing only just half.
See the cups always full
don't let temptations ever exert their pull.
Satisfaction is a gift we can sow
helping us to forever gracefully grow.
Pulling up ourselves if ever low
for there's so much love we already know.

In small wonders of life
there's nothing to strive
just learning to thus thrive
could make you jive.

We got our gifts
may be through different lifts
in varied trans and shifts.
In ways we didn't ask
after completing our task.

Pray Ye bless me in Thy loving ways
as I open my arms every night and day
allowing my heart to joyfully play.
Surrending before Thy might
holding on to You so tight.
Heaving a sigh of relief
allowing myself to completely believe.

Live in the moment, inhaling it's wonders
a song of silence or perhaps a whisper of love
there's nothing more precious
than believing in the God above.
Living in the moment even if friends are few
he has your best and is willing to give the best that may
be due.

# 18. Pashmina

Showing off her colourful Pashmina
was my friend Surina
draped around her shoulders
with designs of flowers and holders.
A pastel Green
with threads with sheen
a different composition
is this shawl of dignified tradition.

Of raw, unspun Wool yarn
obtained from Goats housed in Barns
by her ceremoniously was it worn
when as a minister was she sworn.

Threads in Burgundy weaving through
as the craftsmen had it sew
with patches of shimmery, antique Wool
looking so artistrocratic, was it cool.

Dating back to Harappa and Indus valley

are such fabrics found in Kasmir around every alley.
Initially treasures of the Mughal's
worn as turbans, coats or shawls by them and their
loyal's.
Also parts of wealthy Indian dowries
as women married with their goods carried to new
homes in lorries.
Also once the symbol of French Bourgeois
worn later perhaps by some Colonel Dubeois.

A shawl with Cashmere and Silk blend
wearing at parties is now a trend
wrapped around the neck as stylish scarves
or perhaps worn as stoles are their halves
usually twelve to twenty one microns in diameter
adding to the warmth even when there's a room heater.
In Wintery months of cold and snow
or even when models ramp walk in a row.
Fashion statement indeed it is
a chance to wear it, we never will miss.

Of my childhood days it reminds
reminiscing that vendor who was so kind.
Visiting my home every other afternoon
or morning
when the door bell did sometimes ring.
Bringing bundles of multi colored Pashmina

which I did see with mom and Surina.
Gingerly spreading those yarns of shawls
resting his back against those thick, brick walls.
Pshusia Pinks and Navy Blues
Rusted Orange and other varied hues.
Rolling out his chest of treasures
sparking our wits and our pleasures.
Some with patterns of Horse and carriages
whilst others were woven with scenes of majestic
marriages.
Plains and bolds
as many as he could hold.
Paisley were mom's favorite
storing them as she did in her tall wardrobe
with her Saris and her large, Velvety robes.

Woven traditionally in Ladakh in Wools like Merino and
Lama
adding a touch to the outfit of a little more drama.
Pashmina - oh Pashmina
a source of income and bread
for the weavers working with those delicate threads.

# 19. Rain Drop

Those tiny droplets across my window pane
glittering and falling as it heavily rains.
Announcing a birth, every milli second
there's a new drop and then the second.

Trickling down the transparent window
some small, some large in size
wiping them will not be wise.
Comparisons to life reign supreme
watching them pour on the window as they clean.
Learning so much on life as I do
observing all and sometimes few.

Of Birth and death do they teach
of a life lived as they reach
the bottom of the window pane
when there's nothing left of the previous rain.

Some trickle slowly, yet smoothly
some rush and bounce as they flow loosely.

A translucent White or muddy Brown
laughing and dancing, while few may frown
these rain drops seem to sing a song
of some lovers tale that's oh so long.
Pattering, badging when it pours
so many hearts it soothes and cures.

A doctor in its own right
healing every sound and sight.
Or a wrestler perhaps lifting weights
mending many hearts, opening their gates.

A mile long may be it's length
though some are short but full of strength.
As clouds thunder
bringing such wonder
dropping these pearls
as I feel my curls.

Few falling into stacks of hay
while others croon and prance with gay.
An entire life lived
as their Earthy scent is sniffed.
A freshness so pure and calm
serves as a love filled, pleasant balm
stretching my hands and my arm
as I do, admiring always all their charm.

Born in pretty, Silvery shade
falling on plants as well and every leaf and blade.
Marching, galloping, slowly dropping down
the skies are laden with a heavy crown
it's the latest news in the papers and media, in every city
and in every town.

Till death do us apart they cry
till they stop and may be ready to dry.
Juggling is life's story, they say
hugging each other as they sway
making room for yet another droplet just on its way.

Those tiny droplets across my window pane
falling as they may on every mountain and plain.

# 20. Naga Sadhus (a religious ascetic who has renounced worldly life)

The Naga Sadhus, covered in ashes with matted long hair
and usually naked
to devotion and prayers have they their lives dedicated.
Ascetics in their own rights
care not of what may be their plight.
Carefree and devoted
besmeared with Ash and with Wheat are they coated.
Renouncing pleasures and luxuries
living a life of surrender and no worries.
Divine warriors seeking liberation
knowing the Lord is their only aspiration.
Minimalistic clothing
all other religions are they opposing
supposedly militant in nature
with no care for any stature

usually fighting for Hinduism
following just no other system.
Organized into monastic orders
having each other as supporters,
enduring every season
they never have reasons
to crib or complain
about extreme hot summers or any rain.
In months of the holy Kumbh[1]
leading processions or performing rituals
they roam around as intellectuals.
Bathing in the river Ganges, a sacred bath
to keep them on their revered path
staying away from all greed or wrath.
A spiritual congregation
when it's time for their celebration
to take a dip and cleanse all sins
from head to toe, from chin to shin.

With coiled hair do they share
in unclad bodies, almost bare
their knowledge and stories just so rare.
Protecting Sanatan[2] dharma[3]
remains their so called karma,
protecting sacred sites they do
and also pilgrimage sites quite a few.
Trained in martial arts

and similar other warrior crafts
taking care of Hindu temples
as religious armies they assemble.

Their strength of withstanding extreme cold
comes from the discipline and faith they so sincerely
hold.
Vowing never to marry in life
they live on their own without husband or wives.
Amongst men and women are found
Nagas and Avadhutas[4] standing their grounds.
Post the Kumbh they retreat
what they achieve ain't any easy feat.
Found primarily around Uttarakhand and Uttar Pradesh
they may also be lingering around Madhya Pradesh.
Eating Wheat, Fruits and vegetables
selectivey choosing their edibles
nuts, roots and milk they may consume
a Satwik[5] diet is what many presume.

On my trip to Varanasi
a young sadhu did i see
wearing a long necklace made of pieces of wood
and minimum clothes as he stood
a Naga Sadhu or perhaps the like
such a resemblance did he strike.
Humbly perched, lost in his world

crossing him as I did with my hair curled.

Leading a life of complete liberation
Nagas begin to live soon after their initiation.
Seeking enlightenment is their only aim
try they not for any name or fame
from this big world they have no shame
for play they not any risky game.
Letting go of egos or any identity
living a life of intense sanctity
representing unwavering faith
creating such a distinguishable lot as the Lord saith.

-------------------------------------------------------------------------

-------------------------------------------------------------------------

-------------------------

1.An important Hindu pilgrimage celebrated every 6,12
and 144 years.
2.Eternal
3.Cosmic order
4.Female Naga Sadhus.
5.Virtuous

# 21. An Indian Wedding

This wedding was a massive affair
with so many guests, resembling a fair.
Aunts and uncles of all age groups
enjoying delicacies and hot, Corn soup.


A stage was set
where the bride and groom met
with fountains sprinkling water from their 3 holed jets.
A gala wedding, an extravaganza
while the bridesmaids drafted and sang a romantic
stanza.
Holding a fragrant bed of Roses
under which walked the bride in slow poses
approaching the groom,
wearing a Blue Silken robe weaved on a loom
while the relatives walked to their sides, making enough
room
on a bright, Sunny, Sunday afternoon.

Waiting with eagerness to witness his bride
was he standing there with utmost pride
what a beauty, what a gorgeous sight
wearing a sari in Pink Brocade, as she turned right.

Holding her soft fingers
leading her tenderly up to the stage
this young damsel, about 20 years of age.
Exchanging glances and garlands they did
stealing his Bronze 'Mojris'[1] as the sisters hid.
What a tradition in Hindu weddings
is this fun and game,
where sisters perform this act without a thought or
blame.

A parade of guests
dressed to their best
in solid suits and trousers, with Orange turbans
a true social gathering of rich and royal urbans.
The women in Jacaurds and traditional Saris
while some wore lehengas embroidered with Zari[2].
While the bride and groom were seated on Golden,
elaborate chairs
friends walked in to greet them, with some in pairs.

Decorated with strings of Jasmines and bells

Lillies and Orchids and some ornate shells.
A feast to relish
with flavors so delish.
Baked and roasted delicacies
made only in fantasies
a creamy, Lemon souffle, iced with fresh Mauve pansies,
a lengthy barbeque
with guests waiting their turns in long queues
awaiting their chance to munch on the grills
topped with unique sauces and all those frills.
The mother of the bride
did her grief she hide
behind that pasted grin
and her glass of herbal, hot Gin.
Entertaining the invitees
somewhere in their sweet twenties to nineties
smiling and laughing
while the photographer continued photographing.

The priest was summoned to play his part
so they could stay married, till death do them apart.
Around the sacred fire, chanting mantras
while friends murmered in the backgrounds a song with
an antara.
Walking around seven times
circling the holy fire
with the ringing of bells and melodius chimes.

A ritual is complete
as they feel upbeat
about being married, now living in togetherness
thanking the Alimighty for such extreme blessedness.

An Indian wedding is a gala affair
where moments of joy and love do people share.

-------------------------------------------------------------------------

-------------------------------------------------------------------------

-----------------------

1.A type of handmade leather shoe or slipper that
originated in Northern India or Pakistan.
2.A fine thread of Gold or Silver that is woven into
fabrics making intricate designs.